KU-446-854

PLANET IN PERIL

SUPER STORMS

Cath Senker

WAYLAND

First published in 2014 by Wayland
Copyright © Wayland 2014

Wayland
338 Euston Road
London NW1 3BH

Wayland Australia
Level 17/207 Kent Street
Sydney, NSW 2000

All rights reserved

Editor: Elizabeth Brent
Designer: Ray Bryant
Cover design by Rocket Design (East Anglia) Ltd.
Dewey number: 363.3'492-dc23

ISBN   978 0 7502 8299 4
eBook ISBN   978 0 7502 8536 0

Printed in China

10 9 8 7 6 5 4 3 2 1

LONDON BOROUGH OF WANDSWORTH	
9030 00003 8601 7	
Askews & Holts	29-May-2014
J363.349 JUNIOR NON-	£12.99
	WWX0012298/0001

Picture acknowledgements: All images, including cover image, courtesy of Shutterstock.com except: p5 © Getty Images; p6 © acrylik/iStock Photo; p8 © Stocktrek; p10 © National Geographic/Getty Images; p11 © AFP/Getty Images; p12 © REX/Stewart Cook; p13 (b) © Julie Dermansky/Corbis; p14 © JOSE ALORA JR./epa/Corbis; p15 © JEMA/Xinhua Press/Corbis; p16 © JOHN JAVELLANA / POOL/epa/Corbis; p17 © CAI PANLILIO/ epa/Corbis; p18: © AFP/Getty Images; p19 © REX/Environmental Images/Universal Images Group; p20 © DESMOND BOYLAN/Reuters/Corbis; p21 (t) © Shutterstock/Mishella, (b) © Shutterstock/Daryl Lang; p22 © MCT via Getty Images; p23 (r) © Getty Images; 24 © Shutterstock/Anton Oparin; p25 © JayLazarin; p26 © Erik Simonsen; p27 © EHStock; p28 © AFP/Getty Images

Text acknowledgements: p11 Eyewitness: 'Teen Survivors of Hurricane Katrina Share Their Stories', PBS Newshour, 12 September 2005; p3 Case study: 'Eight years later, Zack Rosenburg continues Katrina rebuilding efforts through St. Bernard Project', Tim Smith, New York Daily News, 30 January 2013; p17 Eyewitness: ; Filipino super-typhoon an ominous warning of climate change impact', Simon Tisdall, The Guardian, 17 February, 2013; p19 Case study: 'Philippine Red Cross volunteers empower communities to prevent the spread of disease', Afrhill Rances and Aradhna Duggal, International Federation of Red Cross and Red Crescent Societies, 15 May 2013; p23 Eyewitness: 'A First-Hand Account: The Super Storm of 2012', Cynthia Roth, EHS Today, 17 December 2012; p25 Expert view: 'The City Resilient', Dr Judith Rodin, Rockefeller Foundation, 23 June 2013; p27 Case study: 'How Math Helped Forecast Hurricane Sandy', Ian Roulstone and John Norbury, Scientific American, 25 July 2013; p29 Expert view: 'Future Disasters: 10 Lessons from Superstorm Sandy', Wynne Parry, LiveScience, 28 January 2013.

The website addresses (URLs) included in this book were valid at the time of going to press. However, it is possible that contents or addresses may change following the publication of this book. No responsibility for any such changes can be accepted by either the author or the Publisher.

Wayland is a division of Hachette Children's Books, an Hachette UK company.
www.hachette.co.uk

Contents

What are super storms?

You've probably experienced a storm with pouring rain, strong winds, thunder and lightning. But a super storm is not just a big storm. It's a massive, destructive tropical cyclone. A tropical cyclone is a severe storm that forms over tropical oceans. When tropical cyclones occur in the North Atlantic Ocean or the eastern North Pacific, they are called hurricanes. In the western North Pacific, they are named typhoons. They are called cyclones in the Indian Ocean.

Eastern North Pacific

Hurricanes

Gulf of Mexico

Caribbean Sea

Tropical North Atlantic

South Pacific Ocean

'DOUGHNUT' IN THE SKY

From above, a tropical cyclone looks like a huge doughnut moving through the sky. That's because in the middle it has a quiet, cloudless centre called the 'eye'. The storm can be up to 2,000 km (more than 1,200 miles) wide, with an eye up to 100 km (62 miles) across. After the arrival of a tropical cyclone, there is calm as the eye passes overhead. Once the eye has moved, the other side of the storm brings renewed high winds and lashing rain.

POWERFUL FORCE

A super storm is far stronger than an ordinary tropical cyclone. It sweeps over islands and peninsulas, and along coastlines. Torrential rains pour down, accompanied by huge thunderstorms. Powerful winds batter the coast, knocking down trees and buildings. The high winds whip up the water so it rises and floods over the land in a storm surge, causing great devastation. A super storm usually lasts around a week. When it reaches a large area of land, it loses energy and soon dies.

Western
North
Pacific

Typhoons

Arabian
Sea

Bay of
Bengal

Cyclones

South
Indian
Ocean

FACT BOX
Why do storms have names?

Meteorologists (experts who study the weather) give names to storms to avoid confusion if there's more than one underway. When the winds reach 63 kilometres per hour (kph) - 39 miles per hour (mph) - the storm becomes a tropical storm and is named. At 119 kph (74 mph), it's a tropical cyclone. In the Atlantic Basin and eastern Pacific, six lists of names are used in rotation, one every year. Each year, the names start with A on that year's list. Pacific storms have Hawaiian names, and there are four sets. Each storm is given the next name on the list, whether it's in the same year or not. If a storm is particularly bad, the name is never used again.

What causes tropical cyclones?

A house destroyed by a typhoon and flood. The floods after a super storm usually cause more damage than the storm itself.

A cyclone usually forms in late summer or early autumn. It starts when the ocean waters are extremely warm — at least 27°C (80°F). Warm, moist air rises from the ocean surface, and condenses to form thunderstorms. The condensation releases heat, warming the air and making it rise.

As it rises, more warm, moist air from the ocean takes its place. Heat continually moves from the ocean to the atmosphere. The movement creates wind; it turns in circles to form a spinning wheel, moving ever faster until it becomes a tropical cyclone.

STORM SCALES

Tropical cyclones are measured in different ways. There are five categories of hurricane strength: category 5 is the most powerful, with wind speeds of more than 250 kph (155 mph). Similar scales are used to measure typhoons. Typhoons become stronger in the western Pacific than hurricanes do in the Atlantic because the Pacific Ocean is much larger, so the typhoons can develop greater power before they hit land.

Season of super storms

2005 was a record year for monster storms. There was a run of 15 Atlantic hurricanes, including the devastating Hurricane Katrina. In total, there were 27 named tropical storms. The meteorologists' list of Atlantic cyclone names ran out and they had to add new ones.

SUPER STORMS AND CLIMATE CHANGE

In recent years, we have seen more frequent and severe tropical cyclones – we call them 'super storms'. Experts link the increase in super storms with climate change. The world is becoming warmer, making tropical cyclones larger and covering greater areas with stronger winds and heavier rainfall. With rising sea levels, coastal regions are more at risk from storm surges. This book looks at three dramatic examples of super storms, their effects and how the affected communities recovered. It considers how technology can help us to predict super storms and reduce their ferocious impact.

On 23 August 2005, a storm begins over the Bahamas, in the Caribbean Sea. It gathers strength, and two days later becomes a tropical storm. Named Katrina, this storm hits Florida, USA, with high winds of 115 kph (70 mph) and heavy rain. Katrina's path continues to the Gulf of Mexico, gaining more energy over the warm waters. By 28 August, Katrina is pounding along with wind speeds of more than 275 kph (170 mph). It is one of the most powerful Atlantic storms ever known. That day, the residents of New Orleans, Louisiana, are warned that a super storm is on its way and are ordered to evacuate the city. Around 1.2 million people flee. Yet tens of thousands of people either cannot leave — they are poor and have no vehicle, or are sick or elderly — or simply refuse to go. The majority are African-Americans.

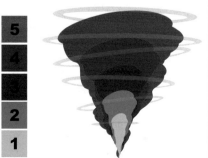

Hurricane category: 4

Maximum wind speed: over 275 kph (170 mph)

The following day, Katrina, now a category 4 hurricane, strikes 70 km (45 miles) south-east of New Orleans. Gulfport and Biloxi, Mississippi, are drenched by a storm surge 8 m (26 feet) high, ruining beachfront buildings.

Eye

Eyewall

hurricane winds spin anti-clockwise'

NEW ORLEANS UNDERWATER

In New Orleans, 25 cm (10 inches) of rain falls – more than three times the average for the whole of August. The city is protected by a levee system of stone embankments (walls) that hold back floodwater. But the levees cannot cope, and many collapse completely. Water gushes over and floods New Orleans. Almost 80 per cent of the city and nearby areas are covered by up to 6 m (20 feet) of water.

Storm surge height:
8 m (26 feet)

Number of people killed:
over 1,800

Number of homes destroyed:
275,000

The economy grinds to a halt

When Hurricane Katrina struck, normal life stopped. Road travel was disrupted, and some bridges were demolished. Oil refineries were flooded, oil rigs damaged and pipelines broken, stopping oil refinery work. Many thousands of people lost their jobs because their workplaces were destroyed. Farming was badly affected as cotton and sugarcane crops were flooded and ruined, as were many forests.

SLOW RESPONSE

Although the USA is one of the richest countries in the world, the authorities' response to the crisis was slow and inadequate. Local officials had either fled themselves, or their buildings and resources were underwater. By 1 September, 25,000 people made homeless by the super storm had sought shelter in the New Orleans Convention Centre, while 30,000 people found refuge in the Louisiana Superdome. A shortage of food and drinking water, in summer temperatures of 32°C (90°F), created a public health emergency at these centres.

Help gradually arrived from other parts of the USA and international organizations. On 2 September, the National Guard (the USA's reserve military force) started to distribute food and water to survivors, and evacuated people remaining in New Orleans. Many countries sent money and supplies, and the Red Cross set up a shelter at the Houston Astrodome, 560 km (350 miles) away in Texas.

Eyewitness

Separated by the storm

'When the storm hit, I was at my cousin's house for the weekend and I didn't know anything about it. . . . I'd left my house at 6.00 that morning. My family, my mom and dad and two sisters, heard about the storm at 8.00 and they went straight to Texas. They couldn't reach me so they told my auntie to watch me. . . .

When the storm came, we went to a hotel and stayed at the hotel for six days. . . . We had food and water, but then the hotel flooded. . . . On the sixth day, we heard that marshals [police officers] were coming to empty the hotel, so we left. . . . We walked through the water to the bridge. . . . A helicopter came and picked us up from the bridge.'

William, 16, New Orleans

Rebuilding New Orleans

After the crisis, a huge clean-up operation began. Canada and Mexico sent troops to help to clear the debris, and the US army brought in huge quantities of sandbags by helicopter to soak up the flooded water in the levees, and made temporary repairs. However, the floodwater in New Orleans did not drain away for several months.

The recovery of New Orleans was extremely slow. Around one million people from the Gulf coast region who had sought refuge in other areas never returned. Only 54 per cent of African-American residents returned, compared to 82 per cent of white people. This was largely because rents on new homes built after the hurricane cost on average 40 per cent more than before. The city has revived though. Tourism has returned, the port is thriving and the convention centre attracts regular business.

BETTER BUILDING AND PREPARATION

The devastation caused by Hurricane Katrina led to an improvement in hurricane protection measures. The old levees had been designed with 'I walls' – straight walls sunk into the ground. The new levees have 'T-walls', with a horizontal concrete base to strengthen them. Human as well as technical failure was also blamed for the disaster. It was clear the emergency management systems had been ineffective. Afterwards, emergency managers improved their preparations to cope with storms. In 2008, Hurricane Gustav put the improvements to the test. After the storm warning, the emergency team successfully evacuated two million people in southern Louisiana. In the event, no major damage was caused to New Orleans, but the effectiveness of preparations had been demonstrated.

Case study

Zack's house-building project

Six months after Hurricane Katrina, Zack Rosenburg was keen to help out. 'We saw people like our family living in attics and out of their cars. They had nothing and nowhere to go.' He set up the St Bernard Project to help homeowners who couldn't get any assistance from the government or insurance companies to rebuild their homes. The majority were African-Americans, and their homes were badly damaged and worthless. Working out of an industrial park in the ruined Lower Ninth Ward, Zack's project rebuilds 100 homes a year, and has helped people all over New Orleans.

It is 4 December 2012. Category 5 Super-typhoon Bopha hits the southern island of Mindanao in the Philippines at wind speeds of 175 kph (110 mph). Gusts of wind rip off rooftops, while heavy rains wash away houses, roads and bridges and provoke landslides and mudslides. On the coast, fishing boats are destroyed.

There is extensive flooding in many communities. Worst hit are the agricultural provinces of Compostela and Davao Oriental, where cornfields and banana plantations are ruined. Tens of thousands of coconut trees topple to the ground. This is the deadliest typhoon of the year.

The death toll is around 1,100 and more than 800 people are missing. Many fishermen were out at sea when the storm hit and perished. More than 210,000 houses have been demolished, and nearly one million people are taking refuge in temporary shelters and evacuation centres.

A TYPHOON-PRONE REGION

The islands of the Philippines lie in the western Pacific Ocean, a disaster-prone area. The country is typically hit by 20 typhoons each year, including three super typhoons – although they usually strike further north. As with hurricanes, when winds reach a speed of 119 kph (74 mph), the storm is defined as a typhoon.

Experts see Typhoon Bopha as evidence of climate change because it affected Eastern Mindanao, an area normally spared. It appears climate change may be extending the area that is affected by typhoons. The five most damaging typhoons in the Philippines have all happened since 1990. Typhoon Bopha was the most powerful in decades.

PREPARATION SAVES LIVES

Although hundreds died in this super storm, many people survived because of the lessons they learnt during Typhoon Washi, which killed 1,200 the previous year. They had been trained in disaster risk reduction. People living along the riverbanks received an early warning two days before the typhoon was due to hit and evacuated their homes. As construction worker Francis Abuhan from Cagayan de Oro, Northern Mindanao, explained, 'The government was well-prepared this time. There were teams of officials going from house to house, using loudspeakers and telling people to evacuate.'

Typhoon category: 5

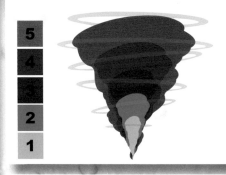

Maximum wind speed: 175 kph (110 mph); gusts of 195 kph (121 mph)

Number of people killed: 1,146

Number of people homeless: 925,412

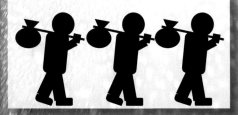

Rapid rescue

Quick thinking by the government allowed many people to escape disaster. Schools were turned into evacuation centres. Local organizations, such as church network Balsa Mindanao, and the National Council of the Philippines, brought food packages to people in Iligan, Northern Mindanao, who were clearing their homes after flooding. Charities, such as the International Committee of the Red Cross (ICRC), provided drinking water, emergency toilets, food, shelter and medical care to more than 273,000 people in the worst-affected areas of Eastern Mindanao. In New Bataan in Compostela, Oxfam and other charities brought emergency toilets and water systems. Their speedy work prevented the outbreak of water-borne diseases such as cholera. Save the Children worked to reunite children with their parents after they were separated from their families during evacuation.

Aid arrives for the people affected by Typhoon Bopha.

On an international level, the EU provided €10 million (£8,429,000) in aid, while Australia, China, Japan and other countries also made donations. The Red Cross and the World Food Programme appealed for contributions to provide food and shelter.

Eyewitness

'We were terrified'

Maria Amparo Jenobiagon lives in New Bataan, Compostela. Typhoon Bopha struck her home in the night, flattening the walls. She and her two daughters and grandchildren had to flee. The only safe place they could think of was the concrete grandstand in the sports stadium. Maria remembers, 'We were terrified. All we could hear was loud crashing. We didn't know what to do. . . Everyone ran to the health centre but houses were being swept away and the water was neck deep. Everywhere we went was full of mud and water. We went to a school but it was flooded, so we came to the stadium.'

LINGERING PROBLEMS

As the winds died down and the floodwaters drained away, some people were able to salvage their homes. But Typhoon Bopha demolished or damaged 216,00 houses, wrecked fishing boats and caused widespread crop destruction (especially of banana and coconut trees), ruining livelihoods and leading to unemployment. One month after the disaster, a United Nations report stated that nearly one million people in the southern Philippines still needed food assistance.

Evacuees from Typhoon Bopha shelter in a baseball court in the southern Philippines.

Rebuilding homes and lives

Six months after the super storm, many people in the worst-affected areas of Compostela Valley and Davao Oriental Mindanao were still in temporary shelters. The ground was littered with uprooted trees, electricity pylons and debris from fallen buildings. Some people who had lost their livelihoods in the disaster remained out of work.

CLIMATE CHANGE AND HUMAN ACTION

As the Philippines rebuilds after Typhoon Bopha, experts warn that extreme weather events are likely to become even more severe because of climate change (see page 7). Human actions can worsen the problems. The population of the Philippines is growing, and people rely too heavily on a few economic activities, such as fishing and coconut farming. So when typhoons ravage fishing boats and coconut trees, large numbers of people are left in poverty. While the country has improved typhoon preparation, these wider issues need to be tackled too.

INTERNATIONAL AID

During 2013, aid agencies offered long-term support to victims of Typhoon Bopha to help them rebuild their lives. The Philippine Red Cross provided materials, tools and advice to people to repair their homes. In summer 2013, it began a project to train 15,000 people to earn a living by becoming carpenters, masons or general labourers, working on the reconstruction of homes.

A voluntary health worker checks the blood pressure of an elderly lady.

Case study

Spreading a health message

Merylin Inongan's home was destroyed by Typhoon Bopha and she lives in a 'tent city'. She speaks the local languages spoken in Compostela Valley and is trusted by the community, as 'one of them'. Merylin has trained as a community health volunteer to teach her friends and neighbours about basic healthcare, first aid and preparing for emergencies. In a future crisis, she will be on hand to provide essential healthcare and advice. She is positive about the future: 'There is a sense of relief when I speak with my community members. Many of us are still traumatized by what we experienced when Typhoon Bopha hit our town, but we know things will get better and we will recover from this crisis.'

Super-storm Sandy strikes!

On 19 October 2012, a tropical wind develops in the Caribbean. Within six hours, it strengthens to form a tropical storm. As it moves northwards, Sandy gains energy. On 24 October, its maximum wind speed reaches 130 kph (80 mph), and the storm is upgraded to a hurricane. By the following day, as the eye passes over Jamaica and Cuba, the winds are raging at 177 kph (110 mph). It's a super storm.

POUNDING THE CARIBBEAN

From 24 to 27 October, Super-storm Sandy hits Jamaica, Cuba, Puerto Rico, the Dominican Republic and the Bahamas. In Haiti, 51 cm (20 inches) of rain lashes down in just 24 hours, causing mudslides and making rivers overflow. Roofs are blown off hundreds of houses in Jamaica. In Cuba, 15,000 houses are destroyed, and banana, coffee bean and sugar crops are ruined. Floods damage buildings and bridges in the Dominican Republic.

NEW YORK UNDER THREAT

Realizing the storm is about to strike New York, the mayor (city leader) orders people in the threatened area to evacuate. On 29 October, the super storm strikes land near Atlantic City, New York. It slows, but winds still rage at a fierce 130 kph (about 80 mph).

High-tide dangers

It happens to be full Moon, the time when the pull of the Moon's gravity on the ocean waters is strongest. This makes the high tides 20 per cent higher than usual, and a storm surge of 4.3 m (14 feet) hits New York City. The wall of water and heavy rain flood the streets, subways and electrical system in the heart of the city, and knock down trees and power lines. Wires fall into the water, trees topple on to wires and power transformers explode, causing fires to break out in New York and New Jersey. Super-storm Sandy proves to be the most destructive of the 2012 Atlantic hurricane season.

Typhoon category: 3

Maximum wind speed: 177 kph (110 mph)

Storm surge height: 4.3 m (14 feet)

Number of people killed: more than 200

Number of people homeless: 200,000

After Sandy struck

The destruction was severe in Haiti, where around 60 people died. Widespread flooding added 32,000 to the number of people already homeless since a major earthquake in 2010. The winds blew away thousands of temporary shelters. The floods ruined 70 per cent of the crops in southern Haiti and killed a lot of livestock, worsening the food shortages in this poverty-stricken country. In Cuba, it was reported that the damage to homes would take years to repair, while up to one-third of the valuable coffee crop had been affected.

But the USA suffered the worst of the deaths, injuries and destruction. More than 125 people lost their lives. For about a week after the storm, all air, road and rail transport ground to a halt, and around 8.5 million people had no electricity. The worst damage occurred in New Jersey and New York. In New Jersey, many homes and businesses in Atlantic City were wrecked by the storm surge and much of the city of Hoboken was flooded after the Hudson River swelled over the sea wall.

Eyewitness

Riding out the storm

Cynthia Roth lives in Long Island, New York. She decided not to evacuate her home before the storm. It was big mistake, as she explains:
'By 9 p.m., the house was completely surrounded by water. There was no power and it was scary. . . In the back, in place of the lawn, I had a 7-foot [2-metre]-deep pond . . . More than 791,000 homes were without power on Long Island as of 11.45 p.m., according to the Long Island Power Authority (LIPA), and they warned residents to be prepared to be without power for at least seven to ten days. . . As it turned out, I was without power for three weeks. . .

After staying in the house for a week after the storm, the temperature in the house was 5°C (41°F). . . When I realized I was developing symptoms of hypothermia [life-threatening low body temperature], I knew it was time to leave.'

Flooding after Super-storm Sandy hit New Jersey and New York.

Crisis response

All American Red Cross
Disaster Assistance Is Free

Many international organizations responded to the disaster. Medical and church charities in the USA, such as the American Red Cross, ACTS World Relief and Global Giving, raised money to help their fellow citizens and Caribbean neighbours. In the USA, charity fundraisers were organized to raise money for the relief effort, including the Concert for Sandy Relief on 12 December 2012. International stars such as Paul McCartney, Eric Clapton, Bon Jovi and The Who performed, and the concert raised US $30 million (£19 million).

COUNTING THE COST

Charity contributions were valuable, but the devastation caused by Super-storm Sandy required government involvement. All the affected countries suffered damage to transport, power supplies and buildings. In the USA, property damage was estimated at US $30–50 billion, while lost business was calculated at US $65 billion. In January 2013, the US government agreed to give US $50.5 billion for reconstruction. As part of this, people will receive grants to repair or replace battered homes.

Expert view

Keeping the lights on

Judith Rodin, President of the Rockefeller Foundation, spoke on 24 June 2013 about how to help New York cope with natural disasters. Her organization has recommended:
'Investments to smart grid technology that would . . . delink parts of the electric grid, so that when, for example, equipment was damaged by storm surge in Lower Manhattan, the whole lower part of the island wouldn't be left in the dark.'

REDUCING THE RISKS

As a wealthy country, the USA can learn from the experience of Super-storm Sandy and make changes to reduce the hazards from future storms. In New York City, there are plans to build flood walls along the coast, strengthen the power grid against flood damage and introduce sealable subway doors so water cannot enter the subways. New hospitals will be built with waterproofing for the electrical systems, equipment stored at higher levels and doors that can be sealed. Existing hospitals will adapt to cope with hazards. At Coney Island Hospital, for instance, the Emergency Department is being moved to a higher level. Adopting such measures should limit the impact of future super storms.

Predicting super storms: how technology can help

If we can predict super storms accurately, people can be warned to evacuate from areas at risk. Meteorologists use satellites and aircraft, landfall forecasts and long-term forecasts. They are continually working to improve the technology used in forecasting.

SATELLITES AND AIRCRAFT

Satellites in a fixed position over the Earth provide images of its surface, showing the position of storms and the cloud patterns. Meteorologists can work out the wind speed from these patterns. To find out about a storm's strength and structure, forecasters use high-flying aircraft to drop devices called dropsondes by parachute into the heart of a storm. Dropsondes measure the temperature, pressure and wind speed, relaying the data to the aircraft before splashing into the ocean. Experts use the data from dropsondes in computer modelling to work out how a storm will develop in real life. However, a storm can change unexpectedly – for instance, a tropical storm can switch to a raging super storm – so improvements in technology are still required.

National weather services use the information from satellites and aircraft to predict when a storm will hit land, so they can issue warnings. Long-term forecasts are useful too. Forecasters compile all the relevant information, for example, about winds, rainfall and conditions in the atmosphere, to work out the number of tropical cyclones expected in the coming season. These forecasts are reasonably accurate.

Case study

How maths helped to predict Super-storm Sandy

The long-range forecast for Super-storm Sandy was that it would die out over the Atlantic Ocean. But researchers at the European Centre for Medium-Range Forecasts realized it would be more threatening. Predicting the weather is complicated because there are different weather systems interacting with each other. The group had to work out how two weather systems - one a system of cool air at low pressure, the other of warm, moist air - would coil around each other. They used complicated mathematical equations involving measurements of wind speed, pressure, temperature, air density and humidity from both weather systems. They predicted Super-storm Sandy's landfall in the USA and helped to save lives.

Protection from super storms

In wealthy countries, money is available to improve buildings so they can cope with the impact of a super storm. Since 2000, building codes in the USA have required new buildings in hurricane-prone areas to have protective features. They need to have impact-resistant windows that will not shatter in high winds, hurricane shutters to cover windows, and reinforced doors. Homes should have roof straps that attach the roof to the house with cables down to a concrete slab or the basement.

LOOKING TO THE FUTURE

So what can we do to protect both rich and poor countries from super storms? Many scientists say that limiting climate change is important, for example, by reducing our use of fuels such as gas and oil, which release carbon dioxide into the atmosphere and cause global warming.

Nature can assist too. Oyster reefs help to break up waves, reducing coastal flooding. Inland, wetlands soak up extra water, protecting communities downstream from flooding. By restoring natural elements of our coastlines, we can reduce the risks from super storms. Reversing damage to our environment on a big enough scale to make a difference is one of the greatest challenges of our times. Government programmes have also been introduced to help the large numbers of people living in homes built before 2000. For example, in Florida, people can have a free inspection and receive advice on how to make their home hurricane-proof. They can reinforce the roof, add roof straps and install water barriers. So people in areas likely to be affected by super storms can protect themselves against disaster.

However, in poor countries, such as Haiti, many people live in flimsy wooden shacks or other temporary homes, and the protection of a hurricane-proof house is out of their reach. Accurate prediction and warning of super storms remain their only way of survival.

Expert view

Restore natural protection

Nicole Maher, senior coast scientist on Long Island, New York, explains that 'As a result of development over the centuries, New York City and its surrounding area have lost wetlands and oyster reefs, natural features that once protected the coast from storms. Restoring these features could help make the coast more resilient [able to cope with threat], by, for example, reducing wave velocity [speed] and erosion.'

Volunteers build an oyster reef along the shore in North Carolina, USA, to protect the coast from erosion.

Glossary

atmosphere   The mixture of gases that surrounds the Earth.

cholera   A disease caught from infected water that causes bad diarrhoea and vomiting and often results in death.

climate change   Changes in the Earth's temperature, wind patterns and rainfall, especially the increase in the temperature of the atmosphere that is caused by the increase of certain gases, particularly carbon dioxide.

computer modelling   Using a special computer program to model a real-life situation, such as a storm hitting the coast.

condensation   The process of a gas changing to a liquid, for example, when water vapour (very small drops of liquid in the air) turns into water and makes rain.

cyclone   A severe circular storm that occurs over tropical oceans.

debris   In storms, all the things that have been swept up by the waves, such as wood, household goods and rubbish.

density   The thickness of a solid, liquid or a gas – such as air.

dropsonde   A device that is dropped into a storm to get data about it.

embankment   A wall of stone or earth made to keep water back and stop it from flooding land.

erosion   The wearing away of the land.

evacuation   Moving people from a place of danger to a safer place.

eye   The calm area at the centre of a storm.

forecast   A statement about what will happen in the future, based on information that we have now.

gravity   The force that attracts objects in space towards each other, and that on Earth pulls them towards the centre of the planet, so that things fall to the ground when they are dropped.

humidity   The amount of water in the air.

hurricane   A violent storm with very strong winds, occurring in the North Atlantic Ocean or the eastern North Pacific.

landfall   When something, such as a storm, arrives on land.

landslide   A mass of earth, rock or other material that falls down the slope of a mountain or cliff.

levee   A low wall built at the side of a river to prevent it from flooding.

mason   A person who builds using stone.

meteorologist   A scientist who studies the Earth's atmosphere and its changes, especially for forecasting the weather.

mudslide   A large amount of mud sliding down a mountain, often destroying buildings and injuring or killing people below.

oil refinery   A factory where oil is made pure.

oil rig   A large structure with equipment for getting oil from under the ground or under the sea.

oyster reef   A rock-like structure made in the sea by oysters.

peninsula   An area of land that is almost surrounded by water but is joined to a larger piece of land.

prediction   A statement that says what you think will happen.

reconstruction   Rebuilding something that has been damaged or destroyed.

satellite   An electronic device that is sent into space and moves around the Earth or another planet. It is used for communicating, for example, by radio or television, and for providing information.

storm surge   When high winds whip up the water so it rises and floods over the land.

super storm   A massive, destructive tropical cyclone.

typhoon   A violent tropical storm with very strong winds, occurring in the western North Pacific.

wetlands   Land that is always wet.

Find out more

Books

Non-fiction

Hurricane Katrina by Peggy Caravantes (Core Library, 2013)

Hurricane and Typhoon Alert! by Paul Challen (Crabtree Publishing Co., 2011)

I Survived Hurricane Katrina, 2005 by Lauren Tarshis (Scholastic Paperbacks, 2011)

Superstorm by Rachel Bailey (Core Library, 2013)

The Superstorm Hurricane Sandy by Josh Gregory (Scholastic, 2013)

Superstorm Sandy: A Diary in the Dark by William Westhoven (CreateSpace Independent Publishing Platform, 2012)

Surviving Hurricanes by Elizabeth Raum (Raintree, 2012)

Tornadoes and Superstorms by Gary Jeffrey (Franklin Watts, 2010)

Fiction

Hurricane Boy by Laura Dragon (Pelican Publishing, 2014)

Hurricane Day by Dee Nicholls (MLR Press, 2013)

Zane and the Hurricane: A Story of Katrina by Rodman Philbrick (Blue Sky Press, 2014)

Websites

Animated guide: Hurricanes
http://news.bbc.co.uk/1/hi/sci/tech/4588149.stm
BBC site with guide to hurricanes and cyclones.

CBBC Guide: What is a super-storm?
http://news.bbc.co.uk/cbbcnews/hi/find_out/guides/tech/extreme_weather/newsid_2296000/2296669.stm

CBBC guide to hurricanes, typhoons and cyclones
http://www.bbc.co.uk/newsround/20122403
CBBC site explains hurricanes.

Hurricane Katrina
http://www.metoffice.gov.uk/education/teens/case-studies/katrina
Case study with links to hurricane information.

Teen Survivors of Hurricane Katrina Share Their Stories
http://www.pbs.org/newshour/extra/features/july-dec05/survivors_9-12.html
Two survivors tell their stories.

Videos

Hurricanes: How Hurricane Katrina Formed
http://video.nationalgeographic.co.uk/video/environment/environment-natural-disasters/hurricanes/katrina-formation/
National Geographic

Superstorm New York: What Really Happened
http://natgeotv.com/uk/superstorm-new-york-what-really-happened/videos/hurricane-sandy
National Geographic Channel

Index

PLANET IN PERIL

978-0-7502-8299-4

978-0-7502-8102-7

978-0-7502-8100-3

978-0-7502-8101-0

WAYLAND